AF469238

THIS GUIDE AND WORKBOOK
IS WRITTEN TO ENCOURAGE:

DISCUSSION

COLLABORATION

COMMUNICATION

A FACILITATOR IS RECOMMENDED TO HELP LEAD THE CHILDREN ON EACH ACTIVITY.

QUESTIONS TO START A CONVERSATION:

1. YOUR FEELINGS ABOUT ACTIVITY
2. WHO COULD YOU SHARE THIS WITH?

RECOMMENDED FOR ELEMENTARY GRADE LEVELS.

A NEW WORD WILL BE INTRODUCED EACH OF THE 31 DAYS IN THE GUIDE AND WORKBOOK.

WITH EACH WORD THERE ARE DEFINITIONS, ACTIVITIES AND CHANCES FOR CREATIVE THINKING AND PROBLEM SOLVING.

EDUCATING THE MIND
WITHOUT EDUCATING THE
HEART IS NO EDUCATION
AT ALL,
ARISTOTLE

SOPHIA AND CHARLIE WANT YOU TO ENJOY THIS GUIDE AND WORKBOOK.

COME ALONG WITH THEM TO LEARN HOW YOU CAN MAKE A DIFFERENCE.

START ON ANY PAGE. THERE ARE NO RIGHT OR WRONG ANSWERS!

1 SMILE

WAKING UP IN THE MORNING!

IT'S A NEW DAY!

WE HAVE THE POWER WITHIN OURSELVES TO MAKE IT A GOOD ONE!

2 KINDNESS

THE SMALLEST THINGS
WE DO CAN MAKE
PEOPLE FEEL GOOD!

A DOOR LEADS EITHER
IN OR OUT.

HOLDING THAT DOOR
ALLOWS:

THE PERSON TO EITHER
ENTER BEFORE YOU
OR
EXIT BEFORE YOU.

HAVE YOU EVER TRIED
IT?
TELL US.

____

____

WE ARE SURE YOU
WILL RECEIVE A
"THANK YOU"

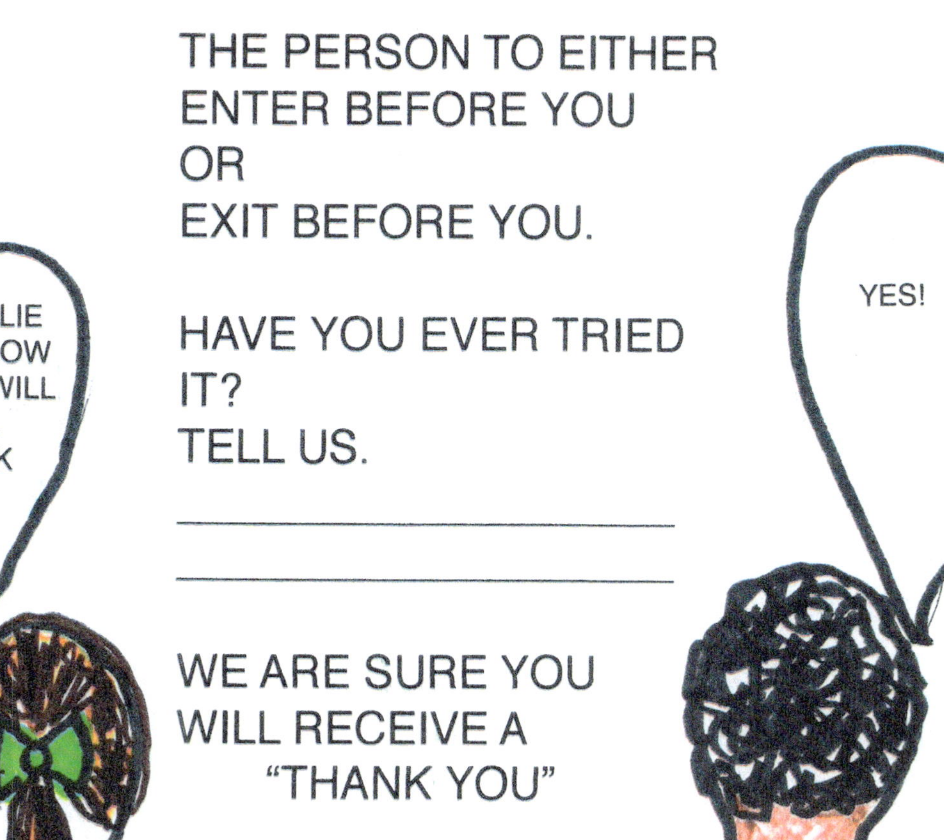

3 ENCOURAGE

EVEN THE OLDEST PERSON AND THE YOUNGEST PERSON APPRECIATES ENCOURAGEMENT!

HOW WOULD YOU ENCOURAGE A:

FRIEND

____

FAMILY MEMBER

____

CLASSMATE

____

NEIGHBOR

____

4 LISTEN

TO HEAR IS ONE OF OUR SENSES.

WHEN WE LISTEN WE HEAR MORE THAN WORDS.

LET'S DO AN EXPERIMENT.

PICK SOMEONE TO LISTEN TO IN PERSON.

LIST WHAT YOU HEAR:

1.
2.
3.
4.

IS IT HAPPY, SAD......

5 THANKS

EVERYDAY THERE ARE A MILLION THINGS WE CAN BE THANKFUL FOR!
AND A MILLION PEOPLE WE CAN SAY "THANK YOU" TO!

HAVE YOU SAID "THANK YOU" TODAY!

LIST THE PEOPLE YOU SAID "THANK YOU TO TODAY.

____

____

____

AND WHO CAN YOU THANK?

____

____

____

6 CLEAN

HOW CLEAN IS YOUR ROOM?
MAYBE YOU HAVE A ROOM
ALL TO YOURSELF
OR
MAYBE YOU SHARE YOUR
ROOM.

HERE IS A CHECK LIST:

- IS YOUR BED MADE?
- ARE YOUR CLOTHES OFF OF THE FLOOR?
- DO YOU HAVE DIRTY DISHES AND GLASSES IN YOUR ROOM?
- ARE YOUR SCHOOL BOOKS AND PAPERS IN ONE PLACE?
- ARE YOUR DIRTY CLOTHES PUT WHERE THEY SHOULD BE?

SAVE

LET'S TALK ABOUT MONEY!
MAYBE YOU GET BIRTHDAY MONEY.
MAYBE YOU GET TOOTH FAIRY MONEY.
MAYBE YOU GET BABY SITTING MONEY.
MAYBE YOU GET AN ALLOWANCE.

SAVE OR NOT TO SAVE....
THAT IS THE QUESTION?

WHICH ONE WOULD YOU CHOOSE AND WHY?
PIGGY BANK
BANK SAVINGS ACCOUNT
OR
ADD SOME OTHERS

____

____

____

8 COMPLIMENT

AN EXPRESSION OF PRAISE COMMENDATION OR ADMIRATION.

GOOD JOB

WHO CAN WE GIVE A COMPLIMENT TO AND MAKE THEM FEEL GOOD?

TEACHERS
PARENTS
FOSTER PARENTS
GRANDPARENT
FRIEND
NEIGHBOR
WHO WOULD YOU SUGGEST?

____

WHAT WOULD YOU SAY?

____

____

____

HOW DO YOU FEEL WHEN YOU GET A COMPLIMENT?

SOPHIA AND I LIKE TO COMPLIMENT OUR TEACHERS!

9 WAIT

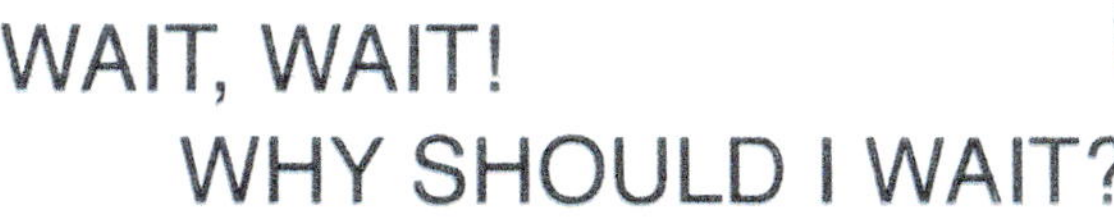

WAIT, WAIT!
WHY SHOULD I WAIT?

MAYBE I SHOULD CONSIDER:
IS IT A GOOD THING?

MAYBE I SHOULD STOP & THINK
BEFORE I RESPOND!

WILL IT HELP?

WILL IT HURT?

WHAT ELSE CAN YOU LIST?

____

____

VISIT

TO VISIT IS TO LEARN

WHERE COULD YOU GO
TO LEARN ABOUT
THE FOLLOWING:

I LIKE TO DRAW

I LIKE HISTORY

I LIKE TO READ

I LIKE ANIMALS

I LIKE SCIENCE

I LIKE SPACE

WHAT DO YOU LIKE?

____

____

ACCEPT

TO ACCEPT IS TO WELCOME PEOPLE, IDEAS. BELIEFS DIFFERENT THAN OURS!

FIND STUDENTS AT SCHOOL THAT YOU WOULD LIKE TO LEARN MORE ABOUT.

YOU MIGHT FIND A NEW FRIEND.

WHO WOULD YOU CHOOSE!

____

____

____

HOW WOULD IT MAKE YOU FEEL?

12 SEW

OH! A BUTTON CAME OFF OF MY SHIRT.

NOW WHAT?

I CAN ASK...

____

____

____

TO SHOW ME HOW TO SEW!

I WILL GIVE IT A TRY!!!!

13 GIVE

TO GIVE IS A SIMPLE ACT
THAT STRETCHES IN MANY
DIRECTIONS!

A RUBBER BAND STARTS
SMALL BUT CAN S T R E T C H!

HOW CAN YOU STRETCH?

WHAT CAN YOU GIVE THEM?

SUPPORT

TIME

ATTENTION

YOU ADD YOUR OWN

____

____

CRY

SOMETIMES WE FEEL SAD
AND WE CRY!

SOMETIMES WE FEEL HAPPY
AND WE CRY!

IT IS OK!

TO TALK TO SOMEONE ABOUT
OUR FEELINGS.

LET'S MAKE A LIST OF PEOPLE
WE CAN TALK TO:

TEACHER

PARENT

WHO CAN YOU ADD?

____

____

____

15 COOK

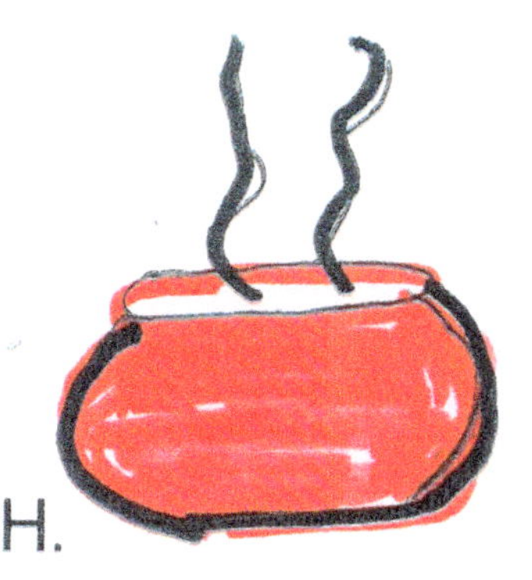

I CAN MAKE A PBJ SANDWICH.

I CAN MAKE SCRAMBLED EGGS.

I CAN MAKE LEMONADE

WHAT CAN YOU COOK?

____

____

IF YOU WANT TO LEARN, WHO CAN YOU ASK TO TEACH YOU?

____

____

DON'T FORGET TO CLEAN UP!

16 INVITE

2:00

RSVP

TO INVITE MEANS TO MAKE A POLITE, FORMAL OR FRIENDLY REQUEST TO (SOMEONE) TO GO SOMEWHERE OR TO DO SOMETHING.

IT'S FUN TO PLAN ACTIVITIES WITH FAMILY AND FRIENDS.

AND IT DOES NOT HAVE TO BE EXPENSIVE.

WHAT WOULD YOU PLAN AND WHO WOULD YOU INVITE?

LAUGH

LAUGHING IS THE BEST MEDICINE!

IT MAKES US HAPPY AND FEELS GOOD!

IT CAN CHANGE SOMEONES MOOD!

IT HELPS US FORGET OUR TROUBLES!

IT HELPS US RELAX!

WHO CAN YOU MAKE LAUGH?

____

____

____

WHERE DO PRETZELS GO ON VACATION?

SPEND

SINCE WE HAVE ALREADY TALKED ABOUT MONEY...

LET'S TALK ABOUT HOW ELSE WE SPEND.

WHAT ABOUT OUR ELECTRONIC DEVICES?

LET'S DO AN EXPERIMENT!

PUT YOUR ELECTRONIC DEVICES DOWN FOR 6 HOURS.

HOW COULD WE SPEND THOSE 6 HOURS?

____

____

____

____

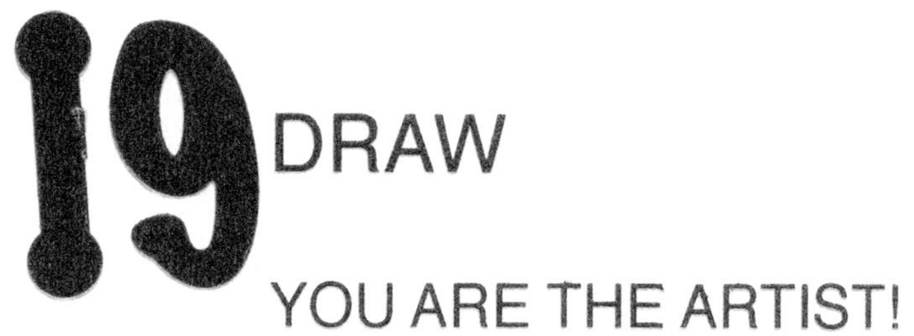

WOW!...THIS IS
BEAUTIFUL!

WHO CAN I GIVE IT TO?

20 HUG

A HUG IS FREE!

A HUG IS CALMING!

A HUG IS SECURITY!

A HUG IS__________

A HUG IS __________

A HUG IS__________

WHO CAN YOU HUG TODAY?

____

____

____

HUGS
FEEL
GOOD!

IT IS UP TO YOU!

MY
GRANDPA
GIVES
BIG HUGS!

21 LEARN

TO GAIN OR ACQUIRE KNOWLEDGE OF OR SKILL, EXPERIENCE OR BEING TAUGHT!

WHO DO YOU KNOW THAT DOES A SKILL THAT YOU WOULD LIKE TO LEARN?

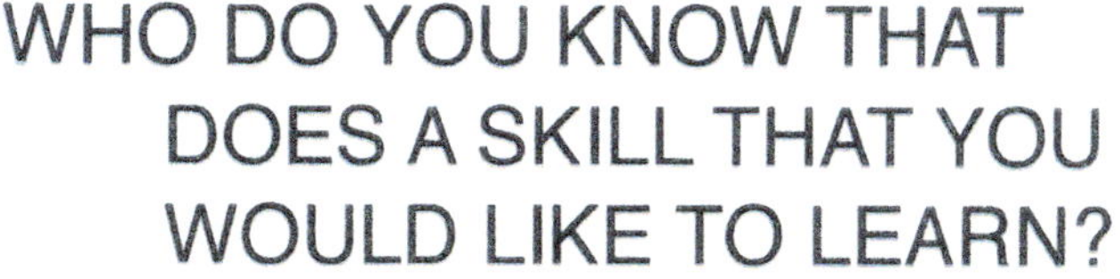

OR WE COULD GO TO THE LIBRARY AND FIND A BOOK OF DIRECTIONS!

WHAT WOULD YOU LIKE TO LEARN?

22 PATIENCE

SOMETIME IT IS VERY
DIFFICULT TO BE PATIENT!

WE WORRY

WE GET EXCITED

WE WANT IT NOW

WE GET ANGRY

WE GET SAD

HAVE YOU EVER BEEN
IMPATIENT?

TELL US !

BAKE

WE REALLY LIKE CAKE,
COOKIES & BROWNIES!

WE ARE SURE YOU KNOW SOMEONE WHO LIKES TO BAKE AND MIGHT LIKE TO TEACH YOU.

YOU WILL LEARN DEFINITIONS, FOLOW DIRECTIONS AND EVEN FRACTIONS!

WHO CAN TEACH YOU?

____

____

____

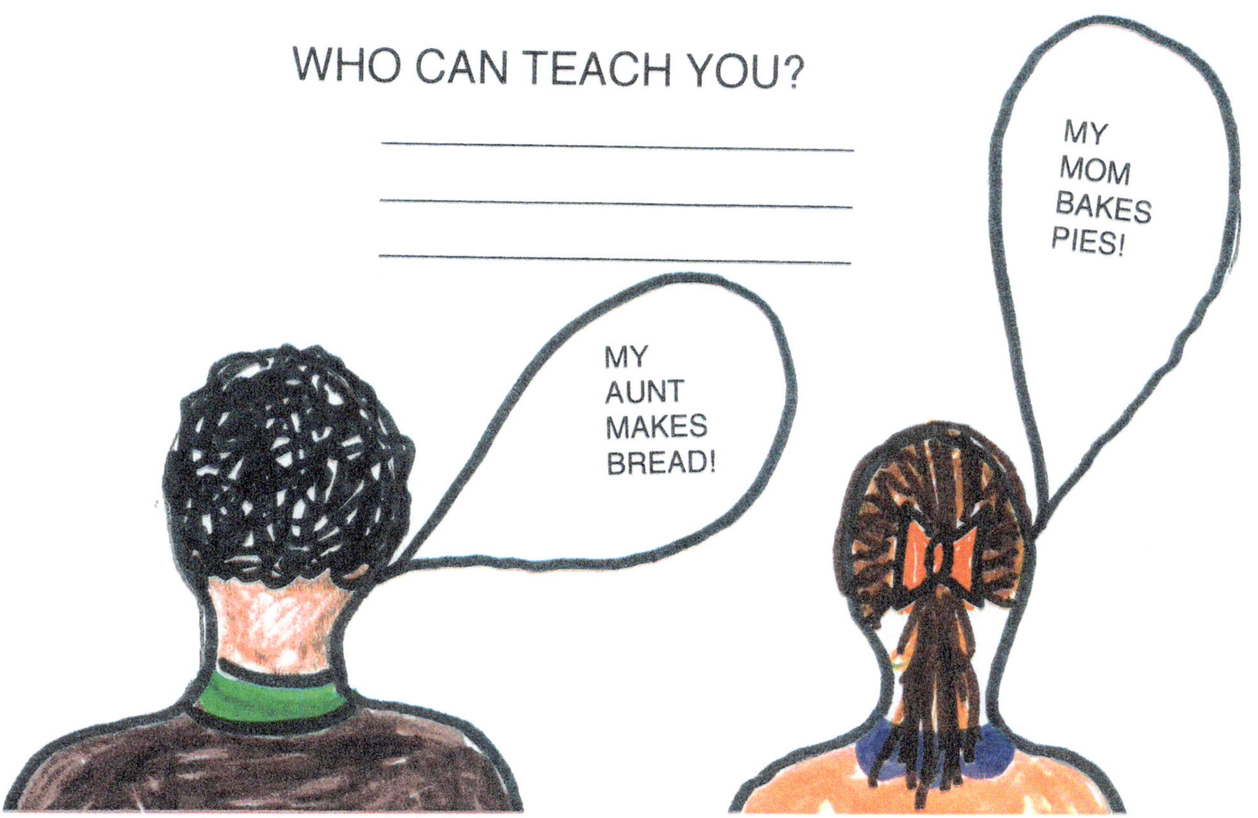

24 COMPETE

TAKE PART IN A CONTEST OR PARTICIPATE!

THERE ARE MANY WAYS YOU CAN COMPETE!

SPORTS & ART
MUSIC & DANCE
4H & DRAMA
SPELLING & MATH & SCIENCE

HAVE YOU COMPETED IN ANY OF THESE?

WHAT DID YOU LEARN?

____

____

____

HAVE YOU EVER COMPETED WITH YOURSELF?

25 VOLUNTEER

TO "GIVE BACK" TO SOMEONE
YOU DON'T KNOW.

HOW DOES IT MAKE YOU FEEL?

______________________________;

____

ANY TIME SPENT
DOES MAKE A DIFFERENCE!

LET'S LIST PLACES YOU CAN
VOLUNTEER.

____

____

____

____

26 CHEER

CHEER UP!

CHEER ON!

CHEER THROUGH!

CHEER JUST BECAUSE!

LET'S WRITE A NOTE AND SEND
IT IN THE USA MAIL!

PAPER, ENVELOPE AND A STAMP
IS ALL YOU NEED!

WHO CAN YOU MAIL A NOTE OF
CHEER TO?

I'LL GET AN ENVELOPE!

____

____

____

I'LL GET A STAMP!

21 SWEEP

TO SWEEP......YOU NEED
A BROOM!

TO SWEEP UP:

- SPILLS
- LEAVES
- GRASS CLIPPINGS
- SNOW
- PET HAIR

WHAT CAN YOU SWEEP?

____

____

1ST - FIND OUT WHERE
THE BROOM LIVES!

TIDY

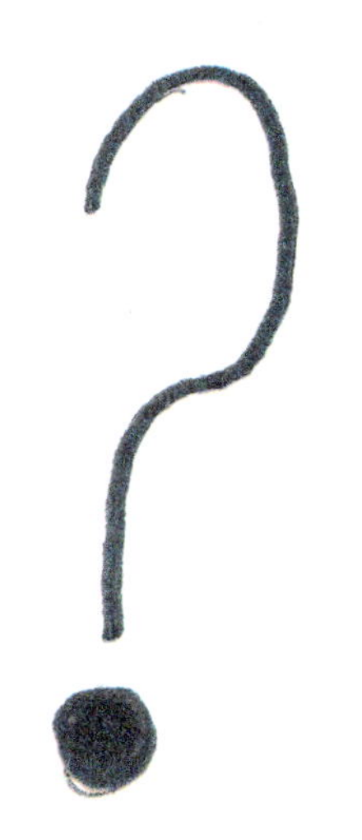

ARRANGE NEATLY IN ORDER!

WITH THAT DEFINITION.

LET'S LIST THINGS WE CAN BE TIDY ABOUT AND TELL WHY!

WORDS

ACTIONS

THOUGHTS

WHAT CAN YOU ADD?

____

____

29 SHARE

WE WOULD LIKE TO TALK ABOUT SHARING IDEAS!

WE WORK WITH OTHERS TO COME UP WITH THE BEST SOLUTIONS!

IF RULES ARE ALREADY IN PLACE LET'S TALK ABOUT WHY THEY ARE IMPORTANT!

SCHOOL RULES

FAMILY RULES

COMMUNITY RULES

NEW IDEAS!

____

____

30 HELP

TO HELP IS TO LOVE!

MAKE A LIST OF WHO
YOU CAN HELP:

____

____

____

____

YOU JUST MADE A DIFFERENCE!

GOOD JOB!

KEEP IT UP!

FOR EVER AND EVER!!!!!!

31 SMILE

WOW, IT'S BEDTIME!

I'M PROUD TO HAVE
DONE MY BEST!

IT WAS EASY!

Printed in Great Britain
by Amazon